CIRCLING AT THE CHAIN'S LENGTH

poems

C. J. Stevens

Published by John Wade, Publisher
P.O. Box 303, Phillips, Maine 04966

Circling at the Chain's Length
Library of Congress Catalog No. 91-65884
ISBN # 0-9623934-5-2 (cloth)
ISBN # 0-9623934-4-4 (paperback)

First Edition

Book production by Comp-Type, Inc., Fort Bragg, CA
Cover design by Heidi Bauman
Printed in the United States of America

ACKNOWLEDGMENTS

I thank the editors of the following publications in which most of these poems first appeared: *Aldebaran, American Weave, Ann Arbor Review, Ante, Apostrophe, Aspect, Barataria, The Barat Review, Butt, The Cambridge Review* (England), *Circus Maximus, College English, Connecticut Fireside, The Crescent, The Cresset* (Canada), *Cronopios, Discourse, Empty Belly, Etc., The Expatriate Review, The Far Point* (Canada), *Film Quarterly, Folio, Forum, Handsel, Hanging Loose, Hollow Spring Review, Hyacinths and Biscuits, Jeopardy, Juice, Kansas Quarterly, The Laurel Review, The Little Review, Loon, Maelstrom, The Midwest Quarterly, Mississippi Valley Review, The Nation, New: American & Canadian Poetry, Northeast Journal, The Panhandler, Pennine Platform* (England), *Poem, Poetry Nottingham* (England), *Poetry Now, Screen Door Review, South Coast Poetry Journal, Stoney Lonesome, Stride* (England), *Twigs, La Voix des Poétes* (France), *West Branch, West Coast Review, Wind,* and *The Windless Orchard.*

Many of these poems have appeared in collections with the following presses: *The Crossing Press, Icarus Press, Juniper Press, Poet & Printer* (England), and *Sparrow Press.*

"Cabin Fever" was published as a postcard poem by *Blue Crow Press.*

Further acknowledgments are made to the publishers of these anthologies: "31 New American Poets," *Hill & Wang, Inc.;* "New Maine Writing," No. 1, *NESPA;* and "It's Only a Movie," *Prentice-Hall.*

CONTENTS

CIRCLING AT THE CHAIN'S LENGTH

JANUARY

I rise from the soft linen
of sleep to find
it's colder.
            January
is stitched to
February on a quilt
of snow, and it will
be weeks before
the threadbare seams
of crust are torn
to shreds.
            Even
last night's wind couldn't
unravel the hem
of icicles along the eaves
or flatten the rumpled blankets
of snowdrifts.
            A daub
of dirty cotton sticks
to the sky, and a tapestry
of frost hangs
in the window.
            I can tell
by the embroidery of
my breath the cold

is here to stay. I must
get dressed.
                There will
be only a small piece
of red lint in
the thermometer today.

BEYOND THE PANTHER

Beyond the panther back
of any morning there is
a land you've never seen
and a way to do the biggest
things and to live by them.
And in one place, one man
can follow the years that come
to him, and be content
with them. And then there is
the man who wants to ride
the panther. He doesn't stay
in one place, but he would be
the first to tell you where
the smallest things are hidden.

HATTIE FARRINGTON

There was always a songbird
swaying on a heavy-
footed tree; always
the heartbeat of
a banging door that kept
some house alive
all night.

And there was
Hattie Farrington—a feather
drifting with the breeze;
drifting through the ironworks
of another battered day.

Now when a songbird
huddles on a bough,
and the immigrant wind
with its alien tongue coaxes
the bird to drop
its feather,

we think of
Hattie Farrington, and say:
The softness of a feather
on the new snow was truly
Hattie's way. Bless
the shape of this morning.

SOMERSAULTS

Somersaults
I made when the clouds
were mine; my feet
had cushions as I
stepped high. I turned
at the top, unwound
like twine; the world
was a ball I could bounce
to the sky.

            Grass was
a heaven I brushed
with my hands, and air
a mountain I learned
to climb. I had
the magic a boy demands
when I went on my walks
heedless of time.

            The world
still topples, but love
for the spill requires
a courage I left
on the ground. If the earth
should fall, it is not mine
to will. I am
still taking walks
but my feet are bound.

A NEW BLUE BIKE

I remember the smell of cut grass
sweetening my tattered pant cuffs
and the magic of daylight clinging
to a new blue bike. Back then
I would skim the *Lewiston Sun*
over the graveled sidewalks and watch
the papers flop like wounded pigeons
as the news of Dunkerque and the Third Reich
postered the doorsteps. Then I
would drop my hands from the handlebars,
whistle, and pump out of sight. Only
a magician's cape of daylight is now
thrown carelessly over the cut grass,
and the *Lewiston Sun* arrives by van.
Hitler is history, and many Dunkerques have come.
But when I least expect to be trapped
by nostalgia, when I am unwilling
to daydream or to become sentimental,
a piece of sky seen in the eye
of a puddle or a bluebird plunging
from a telephone line reminds me
that once there was a time
when a new blue bike was mine.

SUGAR AND SPICE

Thinking of the sugar
and spice ingredients
of girls that frosted the Bible-
school lawn, and watching
the hired girl through the cat's
pupil in the Christian
door—I remember how
one Sunday's coaxing got
a cousin of mine behind
the woodshed. The fumbling
I have long since forgotten,
but even to this day
I can remember the sphinx-
like expression on
my mother's face, and how
she whipped us with a stick
that didn't stop trembling
until it broke to pieces
in her beautiful hands.

PEDDLERS

The man who sold buttons
and threads walked the mud roads
when the birds were building their nests.
This was back in the thirties,
down on the farm. And the man
who bought rags returned
in early May—he was followed
by the brush man, the itinerant preacher,
and the toilet cleaner. In June,
the wandering cobbler appeared,
and the hatter arrived with the hay.
Then came the bouncy seller
of sarsaparilla, the lame allergist
who read palms, the feather merchant,
and the painter of barns. The distiller
of applejack clattered into the yard
on his cart as the apples were being picked.
They always knew what was done or needed;
they came until it snowed: the drifter
who sold blankets and earmuffs during
the first frost, the man with liniments,
the blacksmith, the mender of sleds,
the peddler who had cough drops and peppermints.

TUB AND WASHBOARD

A scene remembered
from my childhood:
a woman is
standing at a tub
and washboard—she is
singing an old song.
The gray in her
long hair reminds me
of willows; willows
hanging in fog
by a stream. A woman
who is rubbing stains—
sweat from an old shirt.
I see her hands
at the yellow washboard.
I look at the chapped sky.
It is morning and summer.
Streets are watered early
to keep the dust down.
She rubs and sings.

DEXTERITY AND COMMON SENSE

Dexterity and common sense
impressed my people more than silver.
"You're only worth as much as your fingers
and the good head upon your shoulders."
That's what my cliché-tormented people
would say. And I grew up fumbling
in my pockets for pieces of tinfoil
and crepe paper. When I was eight,
I hammered a whole keg of spikes
into the stable floor. I must
have been eleven when I butchered
a watch for its gold. Such practices
disturbed the Solomon composure
of my elders. "The boy's wishbone
is where his backbone should be;
see how the gold slips from his fingers!"
That's what my people said. The stable
now rests with a bonnet of spikes
in the uncut grass, and I've kept a watch
for my children's destructive impulses.
I'm wondering what they'll do with their lives.

THE SHACK

Whenever the wind is blowing
and everyone is asleep,
I get thinking I'm inside
an animal. Next morning
I see there are no new
tracks in the clotted snow.
I wasn't carried off
in the belly of the beast.
Mama and Papa are bunched
before the table, and a puddle
of noses steams by the stove.
But Papa, he doesn't stop
talking about the big
houses chained to the hill—
nothing but pets, he tells us.
He doesn't think the world
is getting hungrier
by the minute; he doesn't know
that we've been swallowed whole.

THE CLIFF

Every morning
I say
my poems to the cliff

then follow
the footpath
up the hill to buy

cigarettes and
bread
and sometimes wine

and every morning
the wind says
her poems to the cliff

and the gulls—
the gulls hold out
their beautiful wings.

WAY BACK IN THE COUNTRY WHERE I WAS BORN

Way back in the country where I was born
people didn't care if things remained the same—
the Bible got read and the laundry stayed in the rain.
No one seemed to mind how mad the world became.
Back there, women would pin the washing to a sagging line,
and old men would thumb the almanac for the weather.
No one noticed the world as it crawled in on all four sores.
Back there, people didn't hear its pitiful whine.

WHEN HE WAS YOUNG

When he was young they placed
him gently in a nest of rags
to keep him warm in the cow barn,
and two men built a fire
to melt snow. The cattle
were restless all that night,
and great beams were creaking
in the mow. At dawn
the steaming horses pawed
the drifts. A woman screamed
between two men by the sleigh.
Everyone watched, and no
one spoke to the man
who held the icy reins.
Afterwards a woman
gave him milk and sang.
Nothing was ever said
about the poor woman
who left the warm barn
screaming. He sometimes asks
the woman who sings the same
old songs. She doesn't remember
she says. It's been too long.

UP NORTH

The panting trees will lose
their tongues when it gets cold,
and the honed grass will be
a porcupine asleep.
Up here, you won't be able
to tell the difference
between boulders and sheep.
The empty days slide past
upon a noiseless sleigh,
and from a birdless over-
cast, the flight of snow.
Up north, the mercury
gets down on its stiff knees.
Even the smoke will lay
its head upon the drifts,
and on the grates, the coals
refuse the silent wood.
Then late at night the clocks
will freeze—you wonder why
you live. This far up north
you think you hear the wind,
and it's only your lonesome breath.

THE PASSENGERS

After we eat our bread
drink wine, and go to bed,
we want sleep to slow our breathing.
Side by side, curled under
quilts, we dream. Day after
day our lives whirl round
and round. It makes us dizzy.
Who is to blame? The wheels
must turn. The passengers
get on and hold their breaths.
Each night a carriage creaks
across the dark. Mornings
we face each other wordless.
But in your eyes I read
no hesitation. The wheels
are always taking us further
and further out. When we're young
we don't mind the rocking.
Daylight touches your face.
Under the table, our child
spins until he's dizzy.
Then sits on the bread crumbs.

DAISIES

When it is plucking time for my young son,
and I am Father William and wiser than words,
I won't tell the boy what I know about honeycombs.
We'll sit upstairs and talk sex;
talk about that mysterious thrill
that leaves each blood cell tall
as a sunflower. If he should mention
daisies, I'll say: "Well, there was once
an ancient theory about such things . . ."
then my voice will fade as if I had forgotten.
I won't tell him that saying love-
me and love-me-not is just one
way of pulling a daisy apart.
Let him learn this from some woman
who will want him to make confetti
out of every field in sight. I'll just tell him
that women are wiser than we are
when it comes to the mystery of loving
but of daisies, their knowledge is slight.

A MAN SHOULD LIE GREEN

A man should lie green
where the breast of the world
begins. He should lie
green and expectant as
a new leaf begging
for rain; green
as a weed dancing
a quadrille in a clump
of bluegrass. A man should
think green before a face-
slapped apple
falls. He should
hold each springtime
steady, the way a gully
cups its hands when water
trickles through. The beryl
of his shadow should lie
proudly before him, and he
should stand green. Each step
taken should be
chlorophyllous and light.
The time of ripening
is long for this beast,
and he is inconstant—
unfaithful to the garland
he weaves.

THE SQUALOR

Behind the dunghill where the cattle wallowed
and the ducks nested their eggs in the muck—
that place has been altered. So has the barn
where the horses switched the raisin flies;
where the bull rattled his chain and looked
with mucous eyes at the empty pail.
The squalor is gone: the carted dung is green
on the breathing hill, the mare's tail now ties
the worms, and the sculpture of the new stallion
stands heavily on its tires. One can't bring back
the squalor; can't bring back the sweating bull
swaying behind the heifer, or the red-white map
of afterbirth where the calf was standing.

MAN DRESSED IN RED

Against a background masterpiece of hemlock trees
he stood waiting for me, and I, unable to escape,
saw him mother his gun in his arms until my legs
unbuckled in the snow, and I felt my breastbone

scrape the worthless diamond on the crust.
He looked at me with eyes I thought could pinpoint
all the ballistics of my dread with one shot—
one horrible moment to shatter my forced disguise.

Blinded by warm salt, caged in my corner,
I shook while his gunnery of sight, and jaw
locked in a grin, tempted me to turn sidewards.
I lifted my frozen chin and I smiled at him.

Sensing my fear, he shifted his gun. My shadow
appeared like a mound or a bump upon that hill,
and I stumbled toward him on the run. I was a target
caught in the sights of a love that could kill.

CARTOON

The animated rabbits munching lettuce stare
without suspicion at the hunter. There is nothing to fear
in Technicolor. One image with a wilted ear
seems to wait the inevitable foe; yet unaware

his feast will end in fire, he relishes the leaves.
Bullets riot and shake the purple wood with drama.
Panic and white smoke circle the trees. A panorama
similar to Bull Run in confusion somehow achieves

what we have never made amusing in a war:
Rabbits chasing their heads down a hill without surprise;
stuffing the holes in their fur with motion, as if exercise
had become, miraculously, the hilarious bailor

of protoplasm. The hunter in his piglike stance,
gun cocked and snout poised like a statue, sniffs the air.
He is about to embark skyward, riding the hot glare
of dynamited vengeance while the rabbits dance.

I, who snicker in the theater, wait disaster.
Oh it may come tomorrow with its crimson flashes,
with its piggy dangers and rabbit-hopeful dashes;
it may come like the laugh from the dark without a master.

MUD TIME

I'm going to walk on pins
under the pines; going
to find on a scarf of snow
the needlework of tracks.
I'm not going to play
pig on a mud road
and wallow way back.
I'd rather listen to water
giggling down a brook.
I don't want to follow
a mud road and feel
that drooling mouth of dirt.
I want to drink the maple's
milk and watch the wind
tug at the stem of chimney
smoke. I'm not going to walk
on a road that's muscled with mud.

THE SAWS

We heard the cries of those two men
caught on the saws that summer two days apart.
The moments themselves lost shape
and the day collapsed.

Young fool Moffitt's ferocious laugh
and savagery before his tears,
and Josselyn's inhuman kindness—
taking the rag of his hand with him into the yard.

And in the blindness of mercy,
among the innocent saws,
July screamed her days out on the waste of wood,
hurrying us past disaster
into September and another job.

THE BENJAMINS

Up the mud road, always
alone, the Benjamins fed
on lonesome porcupine, and all
the hidden winter they tribed round
an iron stove, gnawing gristles
and smelling of dough. But spring
trooped them out along the wall
to gawk at accidental cars
that wallowed past like hogs. The smell
of dung and greens rose on the wind's
back for miles. Yet the Benjamins,
slow-footed and sullen, heavy as bread,
had not been herded into believing
a sour wind could dance with a light step.

AGES AGO

Ages ago
the wind buried
the windows with
pillows of snow
and the last stars
were hidden in
a pocket of clouds
then the thunder
of ice rose from
the lake and water
froze in the pipes
and I sat up late
looking back on
all my rages
all my regrets
as the chimney
emptied the stove
then off to bed
with misgivings
feeling helpless
and feeling low
that was last night
ages ago.

FORECAST

The bender of the rainbow is getting wet
behind the slippery hill. The sun
has no more strength than a buttercup.
The stretcher of grass is sad and uneasy—
she wants to warm her skirt before the insects come.
They are all kept waiting:
the flower folders, the ivy spreaders, the seed breakers.
There is going to be more cold weather.
They are all losing patience.
Three more months before it is summer.

DOWNPOUR

Rain crowds
the attic of
the world and slides
down its bannister of
air. Clouds
crack like plaster
on the ceiling of
the sky. We can't
recall the roof of
daylight or
the chimney of
the sun. We find
sticky pearls of
mildew on
the walls. The paired
birds fly up
the wallpaper of
houses and elms.
The carpeting of
the earth is tracked
with mud. Another
end to the world
may be rising to
meet us. Another
flood. By twos
we embark.

TICKTACKTOE

When I became myself I had
to say over and over, "give
your life to a straight line; cross
here and you lose, and if you stay
you gain."

I didn't know once
what it meant to go forward.
So many lines were there to follow:
O's I made, and X's made
by others—not one connecting.

My infant son—it may have nothing
to do with this—my son reaches
and feels where his legs meet, the line
he finds beyond his straight body.
He looks at me. He is fingering
the soft flesh. He doesn't know.

GROGAN

Don't look now but
here comes the man who shakes
the grimy hands of letters
at each door. It is
our Irish postman, the ever-
faithful, conscientious
Grogan. He is a Fyodor
Dostoyevski character.
A real Ivan Ivanovitch
fresh from his Russian landscape
via the open door of
an open book. Ivan Turgenev
would have given this peasant
a nervous disposition
and a litter of pigs. In *War
and Peace*, Grogan would
have been the hostler fetching
oats for a nobleman's horse.
In such a Tolstoyan setting
the Grogans of this world
are soon lost. And here
comes Grogan, saying good-bye
to the world's worries. We are
described in the smudged palm
of each letter.

OTHELLO UP NORTH

Brakeman Lester Emmons was the first
black man to live in our northern town.
He got along with everyone and was well liked
until he married Sam Fletcher's only daughter.
I overheard my uncle say to my mother:
"Pity their little tykes; they'll all be striped."

But Margie's three boys were born nut brown,
and being the only black children around
they were afraid of us whites. They grew
up shy; they always stayed together—
Freddie, David and Dale. "Margie's niggers,"
Sam Fletcher said. No grandchildren of his.

Then one night young Andy Small got drunk,
stole my cousin's car, and raced through town
without a light. David and Dale were only bruised,
but Freddie was dead. "None of this
should have happened," my uncle said.
"Andy would have seen them had they been white."

SAM

There are so many things about Sam
that we don't know: something about the way
he looks at one when saying no,
the pointless shrug and the mechanical shake,
the way he fails to slit his face with a smile
for acceptance, the architecture of his brow
when he is confronted with a mistake—there may be
some rigid rule of self-control that causes Sam
to hesitate; to show no trace of surprise
in the puddles of his eyes. It's only when
the human mechanics of participation
occur to him that we get caught in the gadgetry
of his handshake. We look at him and know
that here is a stranger who lacks our social grace.
A stalled man who is silent when we speak.
It's Sam who comes up missing in the crush of words.
A man who has a blank expression on his face.

MADAM

When madam grows soft
and old and loses
control of her girls
and the whorehouse
is bulldozed into
a parking lot, madam moves
to an efficiency flat. Next morning
madam puts on her bracelets and wears
her glass beads and her lavender shawl.
In K Mart she buys a universe
of tinsel stars, some candles,
a deck of cards, and a goldfish bowl
instead of a crystal ball.
In no time, and one by one,
all the old boys who love madam
are back. Madam
sits holding an old hand
as if it were a crumpled bank note
about to disappear under her blouse.

LANDLADY

punctual as daylight she reappears in the doorway
a nosegay of compliments is thrust into my face
her bonnet tilts upon an overlapping tuft of hay
she begins to nod and sway like a sunflower
she reaches for my money and smooths the minty leaves
I explain the cumbersome realities of plumbing
a sigh of resignation climbs her trellis of breath
she mops a sprinkle of honey from her brow
I wait in her flower dump—stateless and ashamed
she transplants herself like a geranium in the best chair
then she blossoms into a garden of words

HIMSELF

Balancing on a neck that's wedged
between two shoulders, the head
of himself rolls to the edge
but never off its perch
as he acknowledges us.

And we look back and wait
until the pushed drape of
a smile reveals a stair-
case of teeth and himself
bids us to come up from
the head-rolling streets to sit
on words.

And afterwards,
we stand clumped in our tracks
as the shield of thin air
broadens and himself departs.

And difficult as this is
to explain—we know it's true:
when this porch-wide and cornice-
high man clicks out of sight
in tiny puffs of motion,
we must crawl back into
our hollow, everyday
sacks and be ourselves.

HORNED POUTS

I remember two fishermen
shouting obscenities at the moon
while chewing off the heads
of horned pouts with their dull
jackknives.

How marvelously serene:
calm pond, flat-bottomed boat.
Moonlight had dusted silver across
the pine groves; scattered tinsel
where the boat slit open the pond's
cool throat.

The proportions were all
in place: moonlight had been planted,
hills draped over hills, the trees
were all in line waiting to be slaughtered,
and horned pouts were flapping
their soft bellies on the water.

RINGMORE

Two centuries back could be now—the town
is asleep. There are no faces blossoming
where the sun bounces from window to street;
there are no voices in the air
this Devonshire day. A maple, uprooted
by a sentry grave, is spilling its last leaf.
Over the cropped grass, over the crossing,
down the brick path to the empty dustbins,
a solitary leaf is tinting its way
across an English day, two centuries back.

OUT OF MIND

Next week a flat street instead of these hills.
Pancake Holland and an Amsterdam night
and the hills of Devon will be lost—out of mind.
I won't be the same man. You won't find me
walking here; watching the tide ascend.
In some new place you will find me altered—
perhaps more solemn as I climb the stairs
or hear the streetcar's imitation surf.
I won't be living by cliffs in the Lowlands.
I won't be hearing the gulls in my half sleep.

WATERCOLOR

On a brick street
I stand waiting
for the next tram.
The yellow cars
will come. Blossom
from nowhere. I'll
get on thinking:
Oh what a day!
In Holland it's
always raining.
On every street
a flower stand.
Big broad blossoms
waving goodbye.
Now it's coming:
that yellow tram
streaked with soft rain.

THE ROBOT BAND

In a honky-tonk palace where the tourists
drink cold beer, I found them on a stage
of gold: four hard musicians in a trance
of steel; four robots playing a dead tune
for the dead guests who were traveling on
to see a tulip show. Picasso notes
hived like bees on the blue drapes above
the robot heads. No colder jazz could be had
in this cold age. I watched the drummer's eyes:
the centers were not black—they were copper screws.
And the saxophone player's lips were lips
of hose, and two red light bulbs were his cheeks.
The bolted arms and legs kept time with me;
the dead guests swayed on their cloth stems.
We shook like cans in a room of cold beer,
and cars were streaming by for the tulip fields.

THE TRAVELER

I'm sitting in an upstairs bedroom writing a poem
and listening to the trains go up and down the tracks.
The midnight express to Amsterdam sounds hollow;
the wagonlits to Düsseldorf vibrate my writing table.
I wish there were more lighted windows in the trains
and more passengers staring at the night.
Between the cities, I'd dust the land with gold towns
and have poets sitting in their upstairs bedrooms,
writing poems, listening to passenger trains,
and wondering how far a line of poetry travels.

AT THE SISTINE CHAPEL

A young fanatic from God knows where
(was he demented or overcome by the repetition
of his prayers?) laughed and prayed
and hungrily chewed his rosary, grape by grape.
I watched the Vatican guards as they carried him away.

Someone had said: "The Ambassador of Peru
and other dignitaries are expected to visit the chapel.
If the young man is seen, it will prove
immensely embarrassing for the ambassador."

I could not stop imagining the predicament:
would the dignitaries throw back their heads
to forecast the weather on the Sistine ceiling,
and would one of the great men ask if the beads were blessed?

The walls of the Sistine Chapel now escape me—
too much richness and my appreciation rots.
I can still see the young fanatic chewing his grapes,
and I can imagine the tight face of the ambassador,
but my only memory of Michelangelo's ceiling is a sore neck.

THE BEACH

The tourists are out with their one-eyed boxes,
and the sea gulls are painting the red cliffs white.

Down by the wharf,
the girl with the long black hair
is singing a wistful song;
no one seems to notice
her psychedelic pants and her baritone voice.

No one seems to care.

All the fat mamas flesh the background
while fat papas suck their lollipop cigars;
the stench from last week's fishing fleet is in full sail;
a bubbly girl winks back at a half-blind box
and shakes her bottom at the lobster pots.

Out on the the pier, a solitary sea gull
is speckling a green sedan.

No one thinks of Seurat.

The sun-spanked shoulders lose their straps;
the hook of a bra is all fingers and thumbs;

No one minds that.

The bathers sit on the fat beach:
It's a lush land,
a dirty-bird painting,
a big striptease.

TOWN WHERE THE ROAD ENDS

I know of a town that ends
where the woods begin. It's solemn
and green all summer; it's jailed
by trees, and in the winter
it's church white.

And when I
went there to stay, I said
to myself: Down the long wrist
of a road you've come to live;
you will be held gently
in a cupped hand.

But the houses
were bolted to granite foundations
and the fields were handcuffed
by walls and the people were moored
to pedestals of stone.

From a closing hand, up
a long wrist, I fled
before the fist could tighten.
Escaping one grip
I ran willingly to the next.

THIS IS JUST TO SAY

wherever you are I want to thank you
for giving me the wrong directions that day
in upstate New York

because of you
I drove north and missed the turnpike
I never would have spent the night
in St. Albans, Vermont

thank you
for setting back my life one day
because of you I found the slippery roads
through the White Mountains and the building snows
into Maine

it's true
only you made me realize
how dependent I had become on others
and how easily I could get lost on my own
I'm grateful for your carelessness or your ignorance

thank you for being there when I needed you

SOUND ANY GRACE NOTE

Sound any
grace note and the melody
is mine; name
a poor monarch and I
shall set his kingdom
right. I have even
substituted for Julius Caesar
on the Ides of March.
But that was accidental—
I seldom participate if there is
pestilence or assassination.
I prefer to be the recipient
of loving mouths and hands.
I am the only man
who has served a dozen terms
as President of the United States.
All my *faux pas* become
inaudible; I dissolve
all my mistakes. My powers
and youthful adventures supersede
Alexander the Great's.
Rodin's *Thinker* is still
puzzling over a question
I raised. I can keep
my Napoleon image
and not go insane.

DESERTED HOUSE

I squat
in a purgatory
of long grass

while the rain
tunnels to the roots
of my hair.

I'm haunted
by an emptiness
I can't fill.

There is
no breath of wind
in my emptied lungs.

All I do is creak and groan
with the shifting timbers
of my bones.

My screams
have been
torn out.

My stomach
no longer rumbles
with laughter and rows.

All I hear
is the scolding snap of plaster;
plaster that rats can chew.

I can't
even open
my mouth.

I'm going
to throw myself
upon the ground

and let the world
pick up the parts
to burn.

THE EARTHWORM DIGGER

He can find only
a few as they snag
the roots and unravel
in the loam like pieces
of string. But where
a carpet of manure
warms the marsh, he can
loosen them quickly.
Sometimes he forgets
the earth's fabric
has a living weave—into
his bait box go
these odd ends. Some
are thick bits of yarn
and some are cut bands
of thin elastic. In winter
when a caftan of snow
dresses the lake, his catch
can be pulled free from
the ice hole. The mouth
of each fish will be
firmly stitched where the hook
runs deep. It's then
he thinks of the frayed
pieces still hanging
from that rug of dirt,
and how every spadeful
comes up threaded.

MOUSE

All morning you kept
hiding under logs
as I sawed wood.
Your nest and tunnels
were exposed to the sky.
You were on bare ground
when I stalled the chain saw.
Both your forelegs were quivering
in the sawdust, and your back
was broken. Twice, to end
your suffering, I swung
the birch hook. The first swing
missed, but the second
brought blood. Your pointed head
lost its shape, and the tiny chip
of an eye no longer gleamed
like polished obsidian
as you died waving.
I forgot you as I split
the small hill of wood.
Afterwards, I found
clots of clay with traces
of chokecherry and matted hay
in the packed sawdust.
I scuffed these under
with my foot, cleaned

the birch hook, filed
the chain saw, and followed
the path through the woods
where the injured leaves
were waving and falling.

FAIR GAME

I don't care if potatoes look
in every direction to stay alive
in their nest   I'm not ready
to imagine the suffering
of beets when their blood
sticks to my hands   oranges and lemons
may shine like the sun
but there the resemblance ends
if a cucumber should remind me
of a blind lizard   I'm not going
to be gentle and kind as I peel
its cool skin   and no
I won't be heard protesting
the plight of an onion   it can
be slow-footed and all skin
I'm not going to convince myself
that bananas resemble boats
let someone else try to float them down
a tropical river   I'm not ready
to study wet grapes like a jeweler
or stare into the crater of a cantaloupe
for seeds of pure gold   fair game
can be found wherever I am   my pleasures
have always been those of a killer.

CUPS

I have begun to notice how
my hand finds the snug crook
of their arms as I ignore
their rude yawns—their bellies
are there to be filled. The clothes
they wear insult the eye,
and when they dress plainly
they still appear vulgar.
Their chipped mouths have
a treachery of their own:
those warm lips upon my lips
soon grow cold. And when my hands
can't grasp their slippery skins,
they twist theatrically,
perversely spray, and smash
into a grotesque scattering
with every splinter poised
to cut. Then my feelings
of guilt and loss as I
pick the pieces up. I know
too well the scalding bite
of milk or the saucer
placed upon a tablecloth
like a pedestal. Lately,
I have thought of myself
beside a stream with my hands
performing a miracle. I am
lifting the gift of water
to my mouth without their help.

SLOW LIMPING

Nobody saw him, the lame man,
but still we knew he had come looking.
Across the wet snow, skirting
the fence along the stiff brook,
he must have found it slow limping.

It looked crazy: seeing one foot-
print packed solidly out of sight
and a dragged log bumping behind.
It seemed that way to us that morning
while we were standing in the snow:

we had been laughing, all crippled up
trying to run; the lame man's trail
had melted some, but not enough
to cave in the tracks of his limping.
And there we stood, helplessly looking,

trying to stand straighter in the path.
We brushed off snow that stuck to us
and walked foolishly single file
all the way back. It wasn't easy.
He must have found it slow limping.

BEHIND BUILDINGS

Behind buildings there is that space
where baseballs and tins accumulate;
where the knees of the wind touch the grass,
and frost creeps in to lie down like a skunk.
In just such a place, the tomcats sleep,
and the fox-trotting mice get carelessly fat.
Beyond, the world goes on with its picked-up pace
as the peg leg rain limps through this cluttered land.
It's here the hobos come to camp,
and lovers dump their hearts upon the ground.

WINTER SONG

Now I lace my boots and bundle
my shoulders in sheepskin and knot
doeskin around my throat and saddle
my head with beaver and slowly buckle
the rawhide strap.

I'm ready to straddle
drifts; eager to stand in my tracks
and to sniff this mountain air.

I'm ready
to shake hands with the wind
and answer the telephone wires
screaming between poles.

And the clothes I wear
will be my fur, and all my tracks
will be a brute's trail.

And I'll wallow
and stumble across the white paunch
of the world.

I won't look back.

UNDER THE SKIN

Just under the skin I've lived a lot;
lived with my pulses, felt my own heart.
Just under the skin my hands perform—
I notice the muscles that knot my arm.
Just under, under the sweat, I stand up tall—
just feel these fingers that rub together.
Under the skin my fists are doubled;
under the skin the cords are tied.
I'm tied together, just under, under the skin.

THE TUMOR

A miniature doorknob
of flesh buffed red
by the sun with a fold
of slack skin hinged
upon a man's throat—
a benign or malignant
doorway he has learned
to live with?

Though it
sticks out from the walls
and seems permanently
installed, he is able to
ignore it.

He speaks
as if there were no secrets
inside, nothing for him
to fear or hide.

No one
will ever unlock this deformity
or pass beyond the plumb
and watertight construction
to prowl the flesh within.

He may at times sense
its presence, but he
wears it as if it were
some misplaced finger or toe.

Perhaps a trick, or the freak
behavior of cells seeking
revenge.

                    If this door
could be unlocked, the tumor
swung back, opening a crack, revealing
a danger, a flaw, my fear
or his lack,

                         would he
be surprised? Concerned?
Would I be content?

I think of this whenever
I look at him; whenever
I worry about myself.

FLOYD

When Floyd talked about God at Mac's Garage,
the Almighty resembled some machine mechanics
could take apart.
If you knew engines better than most,
you had that saintliness Floyd wheezed about.
After plugs, grease, gas and oil,
he spoke of the differential, clutch and coil—
God Almighty stripped down, scattered over the floor
at Mac's.
And Floyd, sitting on a Buick seat outside,
would smile as the boys pumped the juices of life
into the mouths of his beautiful friends.
Floyd would rave and mumble predictions.
Then he would chuckle as he studied the world of tin.

ALEX

I knew Alex Goldsmith
when he was old. Laughter
didn't crease the leather
of his face. His eyes
and light-blue lips
were his credentials of wit.
A hackmatack would best
describe his soul. Rooted
to earth he lived in a climate
of autumn. Trees were slowly
uprooted around him.
The smell of snow was in
the air when I knew him,
and often we laughed together
because he liked me.

THE UNCLE

He sits in a stuffed chair
and tries to hide a penny
in his thin hair as two
young girls begin to squeal
and pinch his knees. There was
a time he thought such things
could never happen. And now
he's not even shocked when their bodies
interlock and he feels the thin chains
of their arms around him.
He's only their uncle. An old bear
of stains and smells. He's circled
at the chain's length and he knows
the circle well. But what
he doesn't know is there.
A lifetime of familiar ties
has left him callous and only
worldly wise—there is no finesse,
no eagerness beyond his wish
to please. Love is like
the ashes in his pipe. He quickly stands,
shifts them recklessly on his chest,
and like the wounded bear
he is, laughingly hurries them to bed.

FANNY DECKER

There were too many warts
in her church of the stump, but she
believed, and this was enough
for us to blame her. To look
suspiciously at the moon.
We didn't miss that witch
who died believing the hound's
uneasy cry. But when
the empty rocking chairs
were sent rocking, and when
the Sunday wash was on
the Monday line, a few
of her survivors still looked
at us. We didn't tell them
the world had changed in the cracked
looking glass of our eyes.

THE OLD ONE-EYED PUSS

The old one-eyed puss
out in the barn is wearing
a medallion of cobwebs
and a silver pendant made
from a moth's wing. Unable
to field a low-flying bird
or corner a rat, he rummages
among the barn boards until
he finds an upended beetle
or a slow procession of ants.
Since he has lost his alertness
and artistry for the kill,
he becomes a connoisseur
of every glittering, easily trapped
chewable thing. All the bright
candle-eyed cats around
look down on him: they arch
their sleek backs and pounce
at his blind side. They have
no use for this aging puss
with spiders on his breath.
But he responds to their prejudice
with all the dignity
of an indifferent tom—as if
he had other commitments
awaiting him. He shakes his fur;

straightens his kinky tail.
And off he goes, out where
the silver pendants grow
among the tedium of flies.

OUTSIDE

He says he has as much
as he can stand. If there
were more; more time to be
himself; more love to give
to son and wife, he'd find
it meaningless to live
in that stone house. It's night.
Another day has slipped
to sea—reversing the tide.
His wife is asleep. In a dream
his son cries. Something
outside wants to come in.
He says it's the wind, but he knows
it isn't. He tell his wife
it hurts him to be happy.
She doesn't know that some-
thing wants to come in
from outside. It's dark
out there, and he's lonely.

SNAPSHOT OF UNCLES AND AUNTS

Here is a snapshot of uncles and aunts
under a rusting sky. The spill of
sunlight settling on the grill of a Buick
blurs the face of the uncle with the cane—
he died a year after this picture was taken.
A stillness in the hydrangeas has caught
the eye of the portly uncle who is pulling
his suspenders. His look of dismay
is not for the camera—diseases
have taken over. And the aunt
who wears the fur piece will live
to be ninety. The other uncle
scowls at the witless lens; a lens
that measures the moment to wink at him.
Then the two aunts with their heads down
and their arms crossed in fat knots—
they must be thinking of bygone days;
they look so defenseless together.
It's a nineteen-fifty summer's afternoon.
They lean into the picture's center
while the stiff trees behind them
are thick with stalled branches and leaves.

THE OLD DRUNK

The old drunk shrugs
his round shoulders and measures
the street. The trees sway
obediently as he waves
the sword of a finger
and prepares the breeze
for its bivouac in a battalion
of red leaves. The tongue
of his shirttail licks
at his belt and he staggers
and straightens himself. A chewed
toothpick clings to the bottom
slope of his lip as he surveys
the injured sunset with its loose
bandage of clouds. He will soon
be stroking some friendly lamppost
or joining a choir of telephone wires
as the autumn air ripens his face.
His cockeyed stare reduces
the evening shadows to ash.
The whiskey on his breath
is the cure for every sadness
and every ill—if he should
hear the lonesome whispers
of his unlaced boots, he

will answer back. Later,
he will wet himself
and scold the reckless world
for its swaying and shoving.

CABIN FEVER

Your watch runs
down as the out-
of-breath wind prowls
for bare ground and your
stove has decided
to sleep with a log
in its mouth and your
bedroom window has
a beard of ice.
You tell yourself
that soon the robins
will perch on the thin-
wristed limbs and the ghost
of last night's snow
will haunt the roots
of bending trees.
But you have lived
too long in cold
weather to believe
that spring will set
you free, that you
will get out of
your house, or rise
from your lethargy.

THE HILL

One night a hill went to sleep under the stars,
and the next morning when the hill got up
with the sun there were a hundred stone houses
leeched to the hill's brown back.

The hill was too round
to brush the leeches away, too round to scratch.
All day long the hill sat in the sun and frowned
at the crab sea that nipped at its toes.

That night the same stars came out, and the wind
jumped from the cliffs. But that night the wind
didn't laugh. The sea made funny noises,
and the gulls clung to the rocks.

When the sun opened
the door of light the next morning, the leeches
were still there on the hump, and there were
brambles and late blossoms. There were even
a few berries. But the soul of the hill had departed.

AS ALWAYS

As always
or so it often seems,
when someone I care for dies
it rains and the usual
happens. I begin
to imagine a disease,
and things insanely important
get neglected. I open
doors to presences so
clearly felt a heavy sigh
escapes me. Days after,
and for no known reason,
the straw speech of a broom
is comforting. I am
amazed and self-conscious
when spoken to; I am
twisted by replies. And always
it is raining or someone I know
hurts himself.

DECEMBER

December is when
the leaves are dead
and the freeze begins.
It's when the moon
unbuttons its vest
of stars as a shirt-
tail of clouds flaps
in the wind.

                    This is
the month when
the windows glow
like prowling toms;
when the door latches rattle
into speech.

                    December
is when the flames
in a stove unwrap
a gift of birch;
when a lonesome dog
begins to bark,
and someone going home
is cold and walks alone.

THE TOOL SHED

Now I put on my singing robes and chant
new songs—I mean I'm in my rag coat
out here in the tool shed.

Around me on the walls, discarded hoes
and shovels. This seems to be the right place
to stack my elbows on the table.

I've got four candles and a ball-point pen,
and I'm happy to be here; happy to sit
on a hard chair in the cold.

OLD SONG

Nobody knows
just how it goes.
That's the trouble
with an old song.
I hear myself
singing it through,
but the words are
wrong. Nobody
will ever know
the way it was.
And all the songs
are like the words
that fell away—
away from me.
It hurts me now:
just knowing I've
got an old song
buried in me.

PS 3573 .A33 C57 1991
Stevens, C. J., 1927-
Circling at the chain's
length